The Pink Mink

Anders Hanson

Consulting Editor, Diane Craig, M.A./Reading Specialist

Published by ABDO Publishing Company, 4940 Viking Drive, Edina, Minnesota 55435.

Printed in the United States.

Credits
Edited by: Pam Price
Curriculum Coordinator: Nancy Tuminelly
Cover and Interior Design and Production: Mighty Media
Photo Credits: AbleStock, Anders Hanson, Photodisc

Library of Congress Cataloging-in-Publication Data

Hanson, Anders, 1980-
    The pink mink / Anders Hanson.
        p. cm. -- (First rhymes)
    Includes index.
    ISBN 1-59679-509-3 (hardcover)
    ISBN 1-59679-510-7 (paperback)
        1. English language--Rhyme--Juvenile literature. I. Title. II. Series.
PE1517.H3784 2005
808.1--dc22

                                                                    2005048033

SandCastle™ books are created by a professional team of educators, reading specialists, and content developers around five essential components that include phonemic awareness, phonics, vocabulary, text comprehension, and fluency. All books are written, reviewed, and leveled for guided reading and early intervention reading, and designed for use in shared, guided, and independent reading and writing activities to support a balanced approach to literacy instruction.

Let Us Know

After reading the book, SandCastle would like you to tell us your stories about reading. What is your favorite page? Was there something hard that you needed help with? Share the ups and downs of learning to read. We want to hear from you! To get posted on the ABDO Publishing Company Web site, send us e-mail at:

sandcastle@abdopub.com

SandCastle Level: Beginning

drink   **mink**

pink

rink   **wink**

I look at the  .

I see the  .

See the color .

Here is a  .

I see her  .

The drink is good.

The mink is brown.

Pink is a color.

The rink is cold.

Rita can wink.

The Pink Mink

I know a merry
little mink.

16

The merry mink
is very pink.

The pink mink
loves to skate
on a rink.

As he skates
on the rink,
the pink mink
holds a drink.

22

"Don't blink,"
the pink mink
with the drink
said with a wink,
"I'll do the best trick
you've ever seen
on a rink!"

About SandCastle™

A professional team of educators, reading specialists, and content developers created the SandCastle™ series to support young readers as they develop reading skills and strategies and increase their general knowledge. The SandCastle™ series has four levels that correspond to early literacy development in young children. The levels are provided to help teachers and parents select the appropriate books for young readers.

Emerging Readers
(no flags)

Beginning Readers
(1 flag)

Transitional Readers
(2 flags)

Fluent Readers
(3 flags)

These levels are meant only as a guide. All levels are subject to change.

ABDO
Publishing Company

To see a complete list of SandCastle™ books and other nonfiction titles from ABDO Publishing Company, visit www.abdopub.com or contact us at:
4940 Viking Drive, Edina, Minnesota 55435 • 1-800-800-1312 • fax: 1-952-831-1632